The Story behind The Story

Story

Butterfly Warrior

An Inspired Memoir By

Shennette Sparkes

ISBN-13: 978-0-9996885-0-2

The Story Behind the Story Butterfly Warrior

For permission requests, please contact the author via the "Contact" page on the following website: www.shennettesparkes.com.

Dedication

This book is dedicated to my miracle
baby, Princess Kyla Nicole Sparkes.
I pray you always DREAM BIG and
believe in God!
Remember to be Bold!
Be beautiful and be who you were created
to be.
I love you so much!

Table of Contents

Forward

On wings like eagles do we fly, high up
into the sky
Trying to get rid of all life's hurts, pains,
goodbyes.
Living a life which seems impossible to
bare,
Overcoming every obstacle while
conquering giants fears.
Knowing that in God I will thrive,
Understanding in life only the strong will
survive.

What is Lupus?

Lupus is a chronic illness that affects over 5.5 million people worldwide. Currently, over 1.5 million people suffer with Lupus in the United States, 100,000 being Floridians. Lupus is a chronic, autoimmune disease that can damage any part of the body including skin, joints, and any organ system including but not limited to the heart, kidneys, and brain. Lupus is known as one of the cruelest, most mysterious disease on earth. It strikes without warning and has unpredictable, sometimes fatal effect.

Each person living with lupus experiences this complex disease in a singular way. Even with its far-reaching impact, Lupus research has been long underfunded and overlooked by many in the medical community. The lack of knowledge and awareness about this disease has left many to suffer silently.   According to the Lupus Foundation of American, Lupus affects 1 out of every 185 Americans, and it's predicted that 1 out of every 250 Americans will develop Lupus.

Alarmingly, 90% of the people with Lupus are women. There is no cure for Lupus, and this disease is one of the most complicated to diagnose because there is no single test that confirms someone has Lupus.   Most cases of Lupus develop during the childbearing years of 15-45. The highest concentration of new cases is between ages 15-22. Thankfully, Lupus is not contagious, and even though it is an autoimmune disease it cannot be sexual transmitted.

Lupus is a disease that is caused by something going wrong with the immune system. The part of the body that fights off invaders such as viruses, bacteria, and other germs known as antibodies starts to attack healthy cells in your body. A number of factors may potentially trigger the disease, including infections, toxins, and environmental factors. Ultraviolet light such as sunlight has been shown to trigger Lupus disease activity in up to 70% of people living with this disease.

Medically, Lupus is classified into five types of Lupus; Lupus Systemic Lupus Erythematosus, Discoid Lupus, Sub-acute Cutaneous Lupus Erythematosus, Drug- Induced Lupus, and NeoNatal Lupus. Diagnosing Lupus can be very difficult because symptoms often come and go. Lupus is also known as the great imitator for many of its symptoms mimic the symptoms of other well-known diseases. Symptoms include but are not limited to painful/swollen joints, muscle pain, unexplained fever, extreme fatigue, red rash on face, butterfly rash, pale/purple fingers or toes, chest pain, hair loss, Edema, Raynaud Disorder, and swollen glands.

Since there is no singular test to confirm Lupus, many patients endure months of testing before being diagnosed. The Alliance for Lupus Research explains that patients must meet 4 out 11 criteria to be diagnosed with Lupus. These criteria are gathered through multiple blood tests, skin or tissue biopsy, and urine tests. A variety of laboratory tests are used to detect physical changes or conditions that occur in patients with Lupus. Patients with Lupus usually see a specialist called a Rheumatologist. According to the America College of Rheumatology (2017), a rheumatologist is an internist or pediatrician who received further training in the diagnosis (detection) and treatment of musculoskeletal disease and systemic autoimmune conditions commonly referred to as rheumatic diseases. These diseases can affect the joints, muscles, or bones causing pain, swelling, stiffness, and deformity.

Autoimmune conditions occur when the immune system sends inflammation to areas of the body when it is not needed, causing damage/symptoms. This type of disease can also affect the eyes, skin, nervous system, and internal organs. The most common diseases treated by rheumatologists
include osteoarthritis, gout, rheumatoid arthritis, chronic back pain, tendinitis, and Lupus.

This book highlights the eight-year Lupus journey of Shennette Sparkes. After years of research, doctors, and testing I have been able to educate and empower myself. Thus, leading to me living a healthier lifestyle and living longer than the doctors thought I would. I moved from pain to promise to conquering Lupus.

Foundations

Self-Confidence
Self-Worth
Self-Esteem

These words should all be based on how we view ourselves. The problem with how most people view themselves is the lens in which they are using. We, as women and girls in a society that teaches us to compete, have lost what a true since of self is. So much of a person's self-esteem and self-worth revolve around what others have to say about them or how others feel about them. So what your hair is curly? So what you are the tallest one in the class? So what your father left your mother? While it might be a scene in the story of your life, those moments should never be the deciding factor of who you are as a person.

When I was a little girl I fell in love with myself because I fell in love with God. God showed me that, despite my current situation or past circumstances, only the strong will survive, so I always relied on him to provide the strength I needed. It was crazy; the more I trusted in him, the more I prayed, the more I cried out to the lord, the more he answered my prayers.

"I can do all things through Christ who strengthens me"

Philippians 4:13

That scripture has always been my favorite, but it really became my motto as a teenager. No matter the adversity. No matter the obstacles! No matter the demons, God has the power to cover it all. I trusted in that and believed it and was tested time and time again.

In eighth grade for about two months we separated from my stepfather. For the first weeks we were forced to live in our car and go to take baths at my grandmother's house until my mom found us a one-bedroom apartment. We were so happy to have somewhere to stay no matter how small. As long as we were all together and safe, that's all that mattered for us. Thankfully this apartment was located across the street from the Nan Knox Boys and Girls Club that we attended everyday after school. These apartments were also three blocks from our church, the New Mount Olive Baptist Church, where we loved to go just experience peace and love. Even though we were going through hell at home, I was blessed to have so many positive outlets. Basketball was my number one outlet. I was able to help lead my team to our county championship going 26-0 that year. I also had straight A's all four semester of my 8th grade year. I was not going to let the confusion in my home stop me from becoming the person I knew I could be.

My junior and senior year of high school my mom battled stage 4 cancer in her throat. They told her she would never talk again. At 16 I faced the fact that I would never get to hear my mom's voice again, cheering me on at games. She has always been my number one fan. I remember always hearing her yell down to me on the court, "get that rebound Sheffield, hands up Sheffield!"

When she wasn't going to be there at my games anymore I wanted to know where was the God I loved so much. Why was he allowing this to happen to my mom? Why now? As I get ready for college, why now? When she has gotten her life together, why now? When she is serving you,

Lord, why now? I had all these questions and I took them to God, as my father. I waited for answers for months. My mom lost her hair, her weight, her passion. I thought I was losing all I had. All we had. She was the only person who loved us unconditionally. The only person who took care of us. I remember watching her. As the oldest daughter, I found myself asking will I do? So I ran, not physically, but mentally, staying so busy all the time.

I was so consumed with fixing everyone else's problems that I had no time to look in the mirror and see that it was really me who needed the fixing. It was me who had become broken and hurt. It was me who was disappointed with God. Wow, that's something to say thinking back to it now, but it was true. I didn't expect my life to end up this way, especially not my senior year. I just wanted to be a normal kid, but normal was never for me. The sooner I realized that the better it has been for me. God created me to be different.

I remember one of my favorite scriptures, Romans 8:28: "and we know that all things work together for the good of those who loved the lord, to those who are the called according to his purpose." As a young girl I always wondered why I didn't like most of the things my friends did, especially girls. I always wondered why it seemed like everyone hated on me or even thought I was "spoiled" because we had nice clothes and shoes, not knowing the amount of work my mother and stepfather did just so we could have anything. I found out then what I know now: most people do judge a book by the cover no matter how clean the cover looks, because society has given us more cameras than mirrors. We spend so much time in life recalling memories instead of creating priceless moments. We constantly search for a standard instead of being the standard.

When my mom was battling cancer she told my brothers and I that if God can get her off crack, no cancer would kill her. When she said that I thought two things to myself:

1. Wow! Crack must be a powerful substance if it made her feel or relate it to cancer.
2. God must be a powerful God if my mom had the faith to believe in him like that.

What I soon realized is that God had set a standard in my mom's life. He had shown his power to her repeatedly and now he was going to show his power through her. Growing up we watched her experience physical and verbal abuse. As a little girl I had heard God's word, even experienced the Holy Spirit, but it wasn't until then that I truly understood the power of God. Just as I had watched cancer take everything away from my mom, I also was able to watch God restore everything and more. My mom's hair grew back, her weight increased, her voice came back to a normal tone, and she has been on fire like never before.

One of my favorite songs, Set a Fire by Will Raegan, has a verse that says:

"Set a fire down in my soul, that I can't contain, that I can't control"

Set A Fire by Will Raegan

That is what God did with my mom. He not only changed her, he transformed her entire life piece by piece. Seeing God do this in my mom's life has always given me confidence. It has always given me the self-esteem because I was able to experience the power of God's love. His love is all we need. It's all I needed as a teenage girl, it's all I needed when my mother battled cancer, it is all I need now as a wife and mother, and it's all I need when battling Lupus. God had set that same standard in me.

During my senior year in high school I was able to obtain a Division 1 scholarship to the University Of North Florida to play basketball. I also received several accolades throughout my community, including the G.E. Weaver Scholarship, Urban League Scholar Athlete Award, 2006 Ford Motors Top Scholar Athlete, 2006 All-State Basketball Team, and 2006 McDonald's All-American Nominee. I was on my way to live my dream, but I had no idea what lay ahead for me.

Story Behind the Story: Butterfly Warrior

Diagnosed

In 2008 after passing out during a post-season workout at UNF, I woke up to find my team and trainer standing over me asking if I was okay. My reply was, "Yes, because Sheff is always good no matter what." You see, as a kid I had learned how to mask and downplay my pain or feelings. I trained myself not to feel certain feelings and emotions, so I wouldn't take on a victim mentality. When things got hard I prayed to God, wrote about it in my journal, and just kept it moving like nothing was happening. Some of it was faith that God would make everything better once I got out of here, but it was also fear of how people who view me. I was always pick on as a kid for being too tall or too skinny but I had no control over that, however I could control these emotions, or so I thought. Little did I know that there was a battle going on inside my body, which would cause it all to change.

After passing out I was sent to several doctors. Some thought I had cancer, others thought I had a thyroid issues, and then finally I was diagnosed with SLE Lupus. This diagnosis explained the joint pain, fatigue, and weigh issue I had but it did not account for the massive lesion that had grown in my head since I was a junior in high school. Whatever it was on my scalp had grown from the size of a dime to now to cover about 1/5 of my head in different spots. It was burning, bleeding, swelling, and I was in so much pain I did not know what to do or who to tell. Just like I learned to cover up my pain earlier in life, I started to do it with Lupus.

I use to go get my hair done monthly just to cover the spots growing in my head. After being diagnosed with SLE lupus by Baptist Rheumatology, I was sent to several doctors about the lesion in my head. Finally, a dermatologist did a biopsy on my scalp and I was diagnosed with a second type of Lupus, DISCOD Lupus. At this point I was weirdly relieved. After many months of needles, blood tests, scans, tests, procedures, and feeling like a lab rat, I finally had an answer.

When my doctor asked me had I ever heard of lupus, I remembered that my friend Jamall in high school had Lupus. It caused him to miss three months of our senior year because he was in the hospital. When he came back he had gained weight and seemed every weak, but no one wanted to bother him so we never asked him questions about Lupus. Now I had to ask myself those same questions I didn't ask then. What is Lupus? How do people get Lupus? What are the Types of Lupus? I needed answers. My life depended on it.

Most of my family and friends were very heartbroken when I was diagnosed with Lupus. No one really knew what the disease was. All they could say was that they knew someone who died from Lupus and they didn't want that to be me. So I decided to educate myself, my family, and my friends on the disease. Despite the fact that not many people know a lot about Lupus, according to the Lupus Foundation of America, over 1.5 million people suffer from it. 100,000 of them are Floridians like myself. Lupus, a chronic autoimmune disease, can damage any part of the body including skin, joints, and any organ system. This includes the heart, kidneys, and brain. Each person living with lupus experiences the disease in a different way. Once I understood the disease better, I was able to help my friends and family understand as well. They were still worried about me, but knowledge is power and knowing what I was dealing with allowed me to begin planning to overcome it.

I remember walking in to tell my coaches at the University of North Florida that I had been diagnosed. I just had left the doctor. I had a new wig because they needed me to do a biopsy with my scalp. I was walking down the hall and my Coach said, "Sheff you changed your hair again." My response was, "Yes ma'am, but this time it is serious." We went into my favorite coaches office, Coach Miller. I took off my wig and for the first time showed my coaches what I had been suffering with. The reason why I changed my hair so much was because over a two year time frame the lesion had grown from the size of a dime to the size of over 50 pennies laying flat on my scalp. I cried because for so long I had been hiding the pain I was in and suffering silently, too strong and too busy to get the help I really needed. Fear had me not wanting to tell anyone.

Shennette Sparkes

As a senior in high school I watched my mother battle stage 4 cancer and my freshman year of college I lost my sweet great grandmother to heart failure. I knew several others with diseases that limited the things they did, and I didn't want anyone to tell me I couldn't go to college or anything so I suffered in silence. Ironically, because I didn't address the issues in my body, things became worse. I had a major flare up. "Flare up" in the lupus community is when you have a sudden increase in activity of antibodies in your system, which can lead to inflammations, infections, many other health issues.

My coaches, teammates, family, and friends were my biggest symbol of hope right after I was diagnosed. After my initial research that told me the basics of the disease, I really tried to research who this disease was but everything I saw was alarming and death. So I decided to stop looking. My coaches promised me that they would help me battle the disease. They told me about another UNF women's basketball player who was diagnosed with Lupus and advised me that if I made adjustments in my life it would be possible to manage this horrible chronic illness. Honestly, I didn't want to just manage this disease; I didn't want to deal with it at all.

Story Behind the Story: Butterfly Warrior

About a week after my diagnosis I had to follow up with my rheumatologist to discuss treatment options. When I met with the rheumatologist I was told the news I didn't want to hear: I was told I should stop playing basketball. The doctor informed me that it would be almost physically impossible to continue to play Division 1 basketball, be a full-time student, and do everything else I was doing while battling Lupus. At that point I told him that I knew that I wanted to continue to play basketball. You see, I had worked since I was eight years old to obtain a scholarship just to go to college. I wanted to make sure my mother didn't have to worry about me. I just needed her to know I would be okay.

Being a young woman of faith, I told my doctor that I was going to continue to play basketball and go to college. I told him, "I worked all my life for this scholarship, and I only have two years left to graduate. We are going to find a way to get through it." I knew that I could do all things through Christ who strengthens. Cancer did not stop my mom and Lupus wasn't going to stop me either. My faith forced the doctors to do something new. For the first time he had to treat a Division 1 athlete committed to competing and chasing her dreams.

We came up with a plan for treatment that consisted of me taking three new medicines long term. One of the medicines was Plaquenil, which over 60% of Lupus patient take to reduce the activity of Lupus in our blood. Another medicine was a steroid. This drug would help with my muscle strength, but it also caused me to gain nearly 50lbs in two years. The last medicine was a type of extra strength Tylenol and Ibuprofen to help with all the inflammation within my joints and help manage my pain. Unfortunately, none of these medicines worked long term.

Story Behind the Story: Butterfly Warrior

Learning to Live with Lupus

Learning to live with Lupus was one of the most challenging times in my life. Due to all the uncertainty and lack of control, I was afraid to face this giant in my life. Never before had I been scared to do anything. Lupus made me second-guess everything around me. It made me question my beauty, it made me questions my strength, but it never made me question my life. When I was 12, I remember going to church with my godmother and great auntie. A lady preached protection over me and told me I would be of great influence one day. She said that I would help change this world. No matter how much pain I experienced with Lupus or how much disappointment I faced in life, I knew God had a purpose for me and it was bigger than anything that I could feel or think. I was bigger than Lupus.

My first treatment plan was working great. I was able to continue to play basketball and continue my studies at UNF. Going into my senior year, I was excited about my last season playing for the Lady Ospreys and we were able to compete for the conference championship. That summer would prove to be a bit more difficult than all the others. Since my body was getting adjusted to my new medicine, I had a minor complication with my menstrual cycle where I bled for 52 day straight. Any woman knows that time of the month when our menstrual cycle on is usually includes a little more anxiety, nervousness, and attitude. Now, imagine dealing with that for 52 days straight while taking two classes and attending summer workouts.

Finally I was rushed to my hematologist who informed me that my hormones were off balance due to the birth control I was on at the time. I then made the decision to go to my OB-GYN and stop talking the birth control. My senior year I joined student government and helped start Fellowship of Christians Athletes on campus. Mid-way through my senior season my right toe began to hurt. At first they thought it was gout because of the Lupus. However, we found out it was just a sprained toe. At that point I was so frustrated with the Lupus thing that I decided to stop taking the medicines and just focus on finishing my senior year. I chose to focus on what I could control and decided to allow God to handle the rest.

One thing I could control was what I ate, and I learned the importance of a healthy diet. Being a little girl from the city, most of my food was fast food and highly processed foods. I had no idea this was a major key to battling Lupus. For years the fast food had allowed unhealthy cells to reproduce in my body. All the sugar and processed food had allowed toxins and other chemicals to pollute my body. Luckily, at the time I didn't drink sodas unless it was with alcohol. Those choices to eat what I want and do what I want began to affect my health and ultimately my life. One of the quotes I learned in school began to resonate with me. "You are what you eat." I thought about it and how it applied to my life. I realized that many of the things I had eaten since I was kid were not good for me mentally or physically. I wasn't getting the proper nutrients or healthy vitamins that my body needed, especially to compete at such a high level athletically.

Even thought I played three sports in high school, no one took the time to teach me the value of proper nutrition and water drinking. Who knew I had been abusing my body by physically depriving it of the nutrients and substances needed to help me have a healthy immune system? I changed my diet and cut back on certain foods that cause ANA (antibodies) levels to rise. My mom purchased me a health journal that dealt with all types of diseases and what causes the disease. Under Lupus there were several factors, including oral contraception and bacterium, which lead to drug-induced Lupus. There was also a section that explained how certain foods, like tomatoes, cause Lupus symptoms to flare up immediately. Changing my diet definitely helped me control my symptoms.

During the winter of 2010, while I was playing semi-professional basketball, I was rushed to the hospital by my best friend after complaining of pain in my stomach. After a CAT and ultrasound of my stomach I was informed that my gall blabber was infected and need to be removed immediately. The doctor warned that if the gall bladder wasn't removed it bust and the toxins could leak out and damage my other organs and possibly lead to my death. I got my gall blabber removed and after recovery went back to my apartment.

After graduating from UNF I decided to stay in Jacksonville. Once my gall blabber was removed I had to stop playing basketball, but I fell in love with Coaching. I started coaching first with the University of North Florida as a student coach, and then went on to help my cousin coach her program with the North Florida Lady Spartans. I got a job working for the Jacksonville Giants as Director of Basketball Operations initially working on summer camps, books for baskets, and their Hoops for Dream program. Eventually, I was able to become a part of the sales and marketing team and help with game day linguistics. At this time I had gotten my lupus under control for the most part. I changed my diet and began to take my meds regularly, I was an assistant basketball coach at a local high school and thought everything was okay.

In 2012 I started to notice that my skin was changing. A little mark had appeared on my face. It was a Lupus lesion on the place I dreaded having it the most: my face. For a long time it was a small lesion, but to me it seemed so much bigger. I would hide my face in pictures or even turn my head for profile pictures. I became so self-conscious about my face, and it was something I never thought about before. Growing up I never dealt with pimples, acne, or anything on my face. I never even drank soda because I didn't want acid marks on my skin, but now I had this spot growing that I could not control.

I went to the dermatologist and he told me that I was photosensitive. I thought to myself, like a plant? But what he meant was that Lupus is photosensitive and the more time I spent in the sun or under UVA lights, the more my Lupus would flare. This made a lot of sense because I had recently started doing athletic training full time along with coaching. This meant that most of my time during the day was under UVA lights in a gym or outside since I did a lot of training in my apartment complex. Helping these young athletes had become my passion and my purpose. I was putting this passion and purpose in front of my own life. I stopped taking trips with my friends because I was coaching. I didn't go to certain events because I was coaching. Sometimes I didn't even go to the doctor because I was coaching. This behavior was all in fear that they would tell me I had to stop coaching.

For the next couple of years I was able to maintain the damage Lupus was doing to my body. I became a teacher with the Duval County

School Board at Ed White High School. With medication and faith I kept it moving. I did what I could do and everything else I left for God to do. He gave me friends who made sure I ate while I was running around coaching and teaching. He gave me my line sisters to be my support, encouragement, and prayer partners doing this time. He gave me young girls and boys to mentor to give me purpose and direction in my life. So I formed Higher Learning Hoops. Higher Learning Hoops is an organization focused on developing the next generation of leaders in the classroom, on the court, and in the community. Our goal is to equip students, parents, and coaches with resources needed for them to be valuable members of society. Higher Learning Hoops also addresses social and civil injustices in our community.

Under Higher Learning Hoops I formed Princess In Pink at Ed White High School to help reduce that rate of teenage pregnancy in Jacksonville, reduce the amount of fights by female students in DCPS, and increase the amount of girls graduating from high school and going to college in Duval County. My first year teaching was amazing, other than the lack of resources, and still we made it happen for our students. Over 35 girls joined Princess In Pink, reducing the numbers of fights by female students on that campus that year by 20%. The busier I got with life, the more I neglected to take care of the simple things. Canceling doctor's appointments to make sure I don't miss practice or class led to my body being overworked and under maintained.

My body began to flare up beyond my control. My husband, who was my boyfriend at the time, would have to assist me in getting out of bed or even taking a shower because of the pain I was in. In October 2013 I was rushed to the hospital. That night the doctor informed us that it was no longer safe for me to live alone and that they didn't know how much longer my body would be able to fight Lupus the way I was living. He told me that if I wanted to have this normal life I would die trying and that I might not even live to see 30 years old. This was a major turning point in everything for me. For the first time I could really understand the seriousness of what I was dealing with. I was not scared of dying, but I was scared of dying without doing the things I felt I was placed on earth to do.

As a little girl I always wanted to write a book to inspire others and own a faith-based youth home/orphanage for at risk youth. Now I wanted to do something to help those with Lupus to not have to suffer silently so I started First Coast Lupus Fight. I met a 17-year-old battling Lupus and coined the term Butterfly Warrior. Being a Butterfly Warrior became my mission. I am a warrior. All my life I had to fight to make it to the top, and now I was in the fight of my life just to live. I decided to educate and empower myself and others about Lupus. I became an advocate with the Lupus Foundation Of America Florida Chapter.

The first year after I was forcing to stop teaching Shakia Brown, a former teacher at Ed White who had lost a friend to Lupus, joined with me to do the 904 Lupus Walk hosted by Princess In Pink. That year we had about 50 people come out. The following year we joined up with Senior Women, a group run by Ms. Bryant who daughter's best friend had been living with Lupus since she was 7. We named the event Laps 4 Lupus and over 100 people came to show support for Lupus awareness. We have held lupus tea party. I have been able to share my Lupus story at a Lupus fashion show, masquerade party, celebration of life, and several churches. My goal with starting First Coast Lupus Fight was to change Lupus from a death sentence to an enteral beacon of hope, giving those suffering silently hope. Who knew this same transformation process would be happening to me on the inside. Last year made the 4ᵗʰ year of the Laps 4 Lupus walk and we had over 300 people attend from Miami, Tallahassee, Orlando, and Jacksonville. We have First Coast Lupus Fight social media, including Instagram and Facebook, as a way to inform people about Lupus, but also to bring unity in the Lupus community by sharing events and other Lupus resources.

Coming to Terms with Lupus

In 2013 I changed my specialists because the ones in Jacksonville seemed to be just medicating me and not actually addressing the issues. The more medicines I took, the more medicines I had to take to deal with the side effects of the original medicines. So I began to see a specialist in Miami, causing me to travel 10 hours a month just to see a doctor.

In 2014 we became pregnant. Dealing with pregnancy and Lupus was the most challenging time of my life. When we first found out we were expecting, my husband and I were excited. My husband more than me because I had read and was told several times that people with Lupus didn't do well during pregnancy. Due to the activity of my Lupus, the doctors suggested we terminate my pregnancy for fear that one or the both of us would not make it through the pregnancy. All I could do was cry. I didn't want to terminate my baby. I remember looking over to the doctor and telling her I have waited all my life to have a child and we are going to have this baby. I will stop coaching, teaching, or watch ever to make sure I could have this baby.

A week later we received a letter in the mail stating that particular doctor could no longer treat me because of the risk I had from continuing on with the pregnancy. I was advised to see a specialist in Jacksonville. At this time we were very confused and I was kind of hurt that at the time I needed her the most, a doctor would just drop me due to risk. Thankfully I was able to get back with my former specialist and I found an OB-GYN who was willing to help us though the pregnancy.

Being pregnant is tough with all the changes in your body and hormones, but I was faced with adding lupus to this complication. In the beginning, my pregnancy was kind of smooth with just a little morning sickness and swollen feet. I was still able to teach and even coach. It wasn't until June 2014 when everything changed. That was one of the hottest summers we had experienced in a while in Florida. Even though I am from South Florida, it was hot in Jacksonville. I was coaching three teams and helping my husband with his boy's team when I could. We were traveling because it was AAU season. After we returned from one of our trips, my family came to see me in Jacksonville.

Anyone who knows me knows I love chicken wings and I love to eat at Hooters, so my family and I went to Hooters. Before we ordered our food, I knew something was wrong. I didn't say anything at first because I didn't want to ruin dinner. I got tired of everyone's plans always having to change because of me. I was tired of us not being able to go places and do certain things because of me. I felt the Lupus had started to limit me and thus limited my family. Once we ordered I told my mom I needed her to go to the restroom with me. We didn't make it inside the restroom. On our way I felt my legs giving way. I grabbed my mom's arm and collapsed. When I opened my eyes I felt my brother and husband picking me up and I heard a woman say, "I am a nurse she needs to go to the hospital!"

Story Behind the Story: Butterfly Warrior

My husband and brother loaded me in the back of the car and we headed to Baptist hospital downtown. When we arrived I was rushed to the back so they could check on the baby's heart rate. A month before we had just had some tests performed on her to insure her heart and lungs were growing correctly. I prayed that nothing was wrong with her. After running a series of test on me they told us I was experiencing preeclampsia. According to the Mayo Clinic, preeclampsia is a pregnancy complication characterized by high blood pressure and signs of damage to another organ system, most often the liver and kidneys. Preeclampsia usually begins after 20 weeks of pregnancy in women whose blood pressure has been normal.

I was in the seventh month of my pregnancy and my kidneys were having serious complications. My blood pressure was 187/121. At that point I was taking about 16 pills and vitamins daily. I was taking 10 medicines to manage the Lupus symptoms and the side effects from the medicines. They had given me medicine to help with heartburn and to increase my appetite, so my daughter wouldn't be underweight. Now I had to add three more pills to this regime. These pills where to reduce my blood pressure, reduce the swelling in my lungs, and to help my kidneys not produce so much protein.

I was also put on bed rest at this time. The doctors warned us that if we wanted this pregnancy to go full term I was going to have to cut out all activities that caused me stress. So I buckled down for the next three months and just focused on preparing to bring Kyla into our world. I began to read and research all I could about parenting and early learning. I also started to set out our house for her. I was excited to be brining a life into this world and I wanted everything to be perfect.

The next couple of times we went to the see our doctors went smoothly. I was going to two doctors a week for the last two months of my pregnancy, my OB-GYN and a high-risk pregnancy doctor. They wanted to make sure my daughter's heart, stomach, and body were developing on schedule and thank God they were. There were no problems with our princess. As we got closer to my due date, I was more and more excited and nervous about the unknown but ready to take on all challenges. I was blessed to have two baby showers with all my family and friends so we had everything we needed for Kyla.

They scheduled to induce my labor at 39 weeks because they didn't want her weight to open my cervix. The week before my scheduled inducing I was having contractions. Because it was my first time being pregnant I couldn't tell if they were Braxton Hicks or real contractions, so we went in and after a couple of hours they allowed us to go home and told me to rest. That next Monday we arrived at the hospital around noon. My induction was scheduled for 2:00. They had to first set up my IV and a line of steroids that I had to have pumped in my body during the entire delivery process. After the IVs and an ultrasound, I was given and epidural.

At about 5:30 or 6:00 they notice that I was dilated, however she was not positioned correctly. They informed us that she was effaced and that my pelvis was pressed against her face, in particular her eyes and nose. My OB-GYN said it was best for us to do a C-section. They didn't want her to choke or not be able to come out naturally. We decided to go with the C-section. I left for the operating room as my husband was given his scrubs to change and prepare to come as well. We were so excited to be about to give birth to our miracle.

When we got to the delivery room the doctors noticed another hurdle. My blood pressure had risen to 181/127, causing the doctors to be concerned about proceeding with the surgery.

Although it seemed like odds were stacking against us, we remained calm, trusting that God had brought us to this place and surely would see us through. My husband grabbed my hand, kissed me on the forehead, and let me know he was here with me and we'd be okay. Before I knew it, she was here. At 7:01pm on September 29, 2014, we finally got to welcome Kyla Nicole Sparkes to the world.

Words can't explain the feeling I felt when I first laid eyes on her. I was just amazed. She was here and healthy. God is so good. I kissed her and then she was off to be cleaned up and checked out. I kissed my husband and he followed behind the doctors, not letting Kyla out of his sight. They took me to the recovery room to monitor my vitals before bringing her down for her first feeding. At first I was scared to try breastfeeding her because several lesions had formed on my breasts during the pregnancy and I didn't want her to affected by it. After being reassured by the doctors that nothing could happen to her I began breastfeeding for the first time. It was more painful than I expected, especially because the lesions. That night after being placed back in my room, I was surprised by my mom and brother, who had arrived at the hospital. Who knew that the whole while I'd been talking to her waiting to go into delivery, she was on Interstate 95 headed to Jacksonville. This was a special moment for my mother. For her, she celebrating her first-born grandchild, the child that doctors told her daughter years ago wasn't possible. The child that doctors said she wouldn't live to see. If that wasn't enough, her birthday was only hours away. That's right, Kyla was born just hours before my mother's birthday.

After a few days of being monitored, we were released to go home. A week later, I was home with Kyla breastfeeding her and started to feel unwell. I felt my temperature rising. Knowing that my husband had just left for work and was headed to practice and not wanting to alarm him or myself, I decided to go lay down with Kyla. I woke up to use the restroom and felt a sharp pain in my uterus area. I was also was sweating a lot. I grabbed Kyla, went into our living room to sit on the couch, and called my husband to let him know I felt something wasn't right. He told me to check my temperature, which was 103. We knew at this time I needed to go back to the emergency room.

As my husband rushed home from practice I begin to prepare for Kyla and I to go to the ER. Since I was breastfeeding at that time, I had to pump to ensure she'd had adequate milk available, as we didn't know what to expect at the hospital. When I arrived at the hospital they did a few blood tests and a scan of my uterus. They determined that the C-section, coupled with a flu shot I received prior to being discharged following her delivery, had caused a uterus infection. They gave me antibiotics, increased my steroid dosage, and released me three days later. From that point on, my recovery from giving birth went rather smooth. My incisions healed, the infection was gone, and I was left to enjoy life with my husband and our miracle.

A couple months went by and I hadn't experienced any major complications from Lupus. At Kyla's 6-month appointment, they ran test to check for Neonatal Lupus. Thankfully, the results came back negative. That was something that I'd prayed a lot about. I never wanted her to have to experience what I did dealing with Lupus. She was healthy and happy. I'd gotten just what I prayed for.

Story Behind the Story: Butterfly Warrior

True Healing

I remember sitting on my floor crying to God about living with Lupus. Some of my lesions had grown together, so I wasn't quite sure how many there were in total, but it was too many for me. Treatment had started to have a real effect on me emotionally. All the chemicals made me feel sluggish and fatigued. Sometimes my throat would burn when I was eating so for fear of feeling pain I wouldn't eat. I didn't want to endure any more pain or more suffering. I was tired of dealing with this uncontrollable disease and I remember God comforting me and telling me everything would be okay. I asked him why me, and his reply was, "Why not you? Just as so many of my great people like Job and Ester had to be tested and what they endured for my sake is why I blessed them the way I did."

I joined Eyes of Fire Ministries in Jacksonville during this time. Going to Bible study on Tuesdays turned into prayer and drenching on Wednesdays. God was strengthening me. He was growing me. He was healing me. In my heart I'd held on to bitterness, brokenness, and unforgiveness and had to remove it to allow me to love wholeheartedly. The next couple of months God moved me from the valley to the wilderness. I was able to spend time understanding more of who I was created to be. At this point I had lost my weight, my hair, and some friends. I lost my job, lost my strength, but never lost my faith.

On the toughest days I'd encourage myself through listening to worship music, reading the Bible, and reading positive things. I read a lot. Reading has always been an outlet and a way for my mind to focus not on negativity. A way for me to escape. I found more hope in empowering others to live. I continued my work with First Cost Lupus Fight as a way to empower those suffering with this disease to be encouraged to live. We continued host events like Laps 4 Lupus,

Hold on to Hope Tea Party, and the Lupus Celebrity Basketball game. I wanted to use these events to spread Lupus awareness and education to those living with Lupus and help provide them different resources to reduce and sometimes eliminate pain and suffering.

In May 2016 I asked my family to go into 30 days of praying and fasting for me to be healed of Lupus. On June 2, 2016 Pastor Tamara at Eyes of Fire Ministries hosted a praying and healing service. I was excited all week to attend. I knew God was up to something. That month had been challenging. The doctors thought the Lupus was attacking my kidneys. I was fed up with all the uncertainty and needed relief. After 30 days of fasting, I went to Eyes of Fire that night to worship. The worship leader called me down for everyone to pray for me. The entire time I was worshipping and thanking God, Pastor Tamara prayed for me. I laid on the floor for about two or three hours feeling the power of the Holy Spirit move through my body. At some point I begin to vomit. Pastor Tamara whispered no more poison and I felt a release in my body. I continued to vomit a little, and then laid down for about another hour. I was resting in the arms of my heavenly father. I hadn't been able to sleep because of pain in my knees, hips, and back, and the medicines made me fatigue. I was just not able to rest, until then.

The next three days I was able to sleep peacefully, and I noticed that my knees and hips weren't in pain like before. About three months went by before I did my blood work again. My nurses and doctor was amazed at my blood because for the first time in eight years my ANA levels were low and the Lupus was inactive. Glory to God! I was so thankful. At that point I chose to stop my treatment because I didn't like the effects the medicines were having on my mental health. Having suicidal thoughts and being depressed was never the standard for me. No matter what I had experienced in my life, I knew God had my back. I knew he was with me and would get me through.

As I journeyed to wholeness, I continued to stand firm in my faith and move forward knowing that one day we would want to have another child. I decided to stop the Cellcypst (chemo) and Benlysta. These medicines are very tough on your body. In 2011, Benlysta became the first medicine approved by FDA to treat Lupus. However, this drug was known to cause deaths in African Americans and takes one year to get out your blood stream. Chemo is similar. Physicians report that for every year you are on chemo it takes two years for the medicine to clear your system.

In 2016 I started a video blog called "Standing Tall with Shennette Sparkes" on YouTube as a way to educate those in the Lupus community on all information I had found and to encourage others to live. On my journey to conquering Lupus I lost my hair, lost my weight, lost some relationships, lost a job, but I never my faith and hope in Christ. As a child being an athlete I knew I could do all things through Christ who gave me strength. I now know what that truly means. God gives you strength to endure the hard times in life, the difficult times. God gives us strength to handle rejection. God gives us strength to handle all we loose.

That strength gives you courage to move forward, to push past all the hurt, pain, and disappointment to get to true healing. This allows forgiveness and unconditional love to be possible. Romans 8:28 tells us that in all things God works for the good of those who love him and who have been called according to his purpose, so I held strong to this truth. I held on to my hope, my faith, and God made me strong. He healed me; he restored my strength because I chose to hope in him. My time with him was my time for him to show me what I was made of. I am a conqueror.

God has won the victory for us through his son dying on the cross.

The Lupus Foundation of America Florida Chapter has this saying, "For a future with no Lupus, we must know Lupus." Being an educator, a couch, and mentor I feel it was not only important that I educate myself about Lupus but also others. I believe in the power of servant leadership. God allows us to endure some challenges in life so we can help others make it through as well. Through this process I learned what didn't kill me made me stronger and wiser, so I am committed to empowering people suffering in silence. I want to encourage them to know no one fights alone. God makes everything possible.

I want others to know that no matter what challenges we have in life, no matter how much we think we have suffered, there is a purpose for it all. Greatness comes with a price. As a young athlete they would tell us "No pain, no gain" and that is a testament to my life. In every area of pain the devil though he was attacking me, but God was exposing what I needed for his next level. To fly higher we must soak deeper. To understand Lupus I had to research and educate myself. To live I had to change my habits, keep my mind positive, and keep moving forward. To survive I had to make up my mind daily that Lupus did not define me.

As a wife, mom, coach, CEO, and author I will continue to serve people and my community. My prayer is that this book empowers you when you face any challenge in your life knowing that "only the strong will survive" and all strength comes from God.

Story Behind the Story: Butterfly Warrior

Author's Note

After eight years of battling this horrible disease, I am thankful that my scars are symbols of hope, that my life is a symbol of strength, and I want this book to be a message of faith. On the next few pages you will find resources on eating healthy while living with Lupus, tips to manage pain, a Lupus glossary, and information on how to contact me. I hope this information blesses you and may God be with you.

Story Behind the Story: Butterfly Warrior

Eating Healthy While Living with Lupus

- Eat foods with anti-inflammatory properties (list provided below).
- Eat food that is easier to digest.
- Eat whole foods or food as close to raw as possible.
- Drink one gallon of water daily.
- Add fish rich in omega 3 fatty acids to your diet.
- Add Calcium products and Vitamin D to your diet.
- Reduce sugar and artificial sweeteners intake. NO SOADS!
- Reduce consumption of trans-fat or mono saturated fats.
- Limit intake of protein-high saturated fat, like red meat.
- Stay away from refined carbohydrates, like white bread, pasta, and packaged snacks.

Anti- Inflammatory Foods:

- Olive oil
- Blue Fish
- Nuts
- Garlic

- Avocados
- Blueberries
- Ginger
- Papaya
- Turmeric
- Cranberries
- Broccoli
- Celery

Vitamins that Promote Healthy Skin
- **Vitamin A**
- **Vitamin B Complex**
- **Vitamin C**
- **Vitamin E**
  Vitamin K

Shennette Sparkes

Tips to Help Manage Pain

- Always think positively. Your attitude will affect your altitude.

- Follow your doctor's orders.

- Take medication on a schedule.

- Follow a strict diet. You are what you eat.

- Limit exposure to sun, UV rays, and black lights.

- Limit caffeine intake.

- Exercise 2-3 times weekly. Exercise helps you maintain strength and a healthy weight.

- Take time to REST. Your body needs sleep to recover.

- Say no. It is okay to communicate openly with your support system about the pain you're feeling.

- Drink water throughout the day.

- Use ice to reduce swelling in joints.

- Use heat to loosen tension in muscles.

- Write down any unusual emotions or pains and contact your doctor immediately.

Lupus glossary

Alopecia Areata - Occurs when the immune system attacks hair follicles, and may be brought on by severe stress. Sudden hair loss that starts with one or more circular bald patches that may overlap.

Antinuclear Antibody (ANA) - Antibodies that connect or bind to the nucleus. This process damages and can destroy the cells.

Arthritis - Joint pain and swelling of two or more joints in which the bones around the joints do not become destroyed.

Autoimmune disease - A disease in which the body produces antibodies that attack its own tissues, leading to the deterioration and in some cases to the destruction of such tissue.

Benlysta - The first medicine approved by the FDA for Lupus. It is a prescription used to treat adults with active Systemic Lupus Erythematosus (SLE) who are receiving other Lupus medicines.

Biopsy - An examination of tissue removed from a living body to discover the presence, cause, or extent of a disease.

Butterfly / Rose / Wolf - Symbols used to represent Lupus.

Butterfly Warrior - The unofficial term for someone who is fighting Lupus.

Chemotherapy - Treatment that uses drugs to stop the growth of cancer cells, either by killing the cells or by stopping them from dividing. Chemotherapy may be given by mouth, injection, or infusion, or on the skin, depending on the type and stage of the disease being treated. It may be given alone or with other treatments, such as surgery, radiation therapy, or biologic therapy.

Chronic Illness - An illness that lasts for a very long time and usually cannot be cured completely, although some illnesses can be controlled or managed through lifestyle.

Chronic Pain - Pain that lasts for more than three months. The pain can become progressively worse and reoccur intermittently, outlasting the usual healing process.

Clinical Trials - Any research study that prospectively assigns human participants or groups of humans to one or more health-related interventions to evaluate the effects on health outcomes.

Dermatology - The branch of medicine dealing with the skin, nails, hair and its diseases. It is a specialty with both medical and surgical aspects.

Discoid Rash - A rash that appears as red, raised disk-shaped patches.

Drug Induced Lupus Erythematosus (DIL or DILE) - An autoimmune disorder (similar to Eystemic Lupuserythematosus [SLE]) caused by chronic use of certain drugs.

Flare Up - A sudden appearance or worsening of the symptoms of a disease or condition.

Hair Loss - Permanent hair loss from the scalp, causing baldness.

Hereditary - Determined by genetic factors and therefore able to be passed on from parents to their offspring or descendants.

Infusion - The slow injection of a substance into a vein or tissue.

Joints - The place at which two things, or separate parts of one thing, are joined or united, either rigidly or in such a way as to permit motion; juncture.

Kidney Disorder - Persistent protein or cellular casts in the urine.

L Hand Sign - Social media campaign encouraging people to put a L for lupus and take pictures with the hashtag #LhandSign.

Lupie - The unofficial name for someone living with lupus.

Lupus Brain Fog - Memory loss and difficulty in processing information.

Lupus Impact Tracker - A list of symptoms of Lupus that you share with your doctor.

Lupus Nephritis - A lupus-related kidney disease.

Malar Rash or Butterfly Rash - A rash over the cheeks and nose, often in the shape of a butterfly.

May - National Lupus Awareness Month.

MRI- Magnetic Resonance Imaging is a diagnostic technique that uses magnetic fields and radio waves to produce a detailed image of the body's soft tissue and bones.

Muscle - A band or bundle of fibrous tissue in a human or animal's body that has the ability to contract, producing movement in or maintaining the position of parts of the body.

Neonatal Lupus - Neonatal Lupus is an uncommon autoimmune disease manifested primarily by cutaneous Lupus lesions and/or congenital heart block. Maternal autoantibodies of the Ro/La family are present in virtually every case, although only approximately 1% of women who have these autoantibodies will have a baby with Neonatal Lupus.

Oral Ulcers - Sores appearing in the mouth.

Photosensitivity - A reaction to sun or light that causes a skin rash to appear or get worse.

Plaquenil or Hydroxychloroquine - An antimalarial drug that lowers the risk of blood clots in people who have Lupus and antiphospholipid antibodies.

POP- National Lupus Awareness Day encouraging people to Put on Purple to show support for Lupus awareness.

Pulmonary Hypertension - Increases pressure in arties connected to the heart and lungs. Can cause shorting of breath, fatigue, chest pain, and a racing heartbeat.

Purple – The official color for Lupus Awareness.

Recovery - A return to a normal state of health, mind, or strength.

Remission - A diminution of the seriousness or intensity of disease or pain; a temporary recovery.

Rest - Allow one to be inactive in order to regain strength, health, or energy.

Rheumatology - A sub-specialty in internal medicine devoted to the diagnosis and therapy of rheumatic diseases.

SLE - Systemic Lupus Erythematosus.

Subacute Cutaneous Lupus Erythematosus (SCLE) - A clinically distinct subset of cases of **Lupus Erythematosus** that is most often present in white women aged 15 to 40, consisting of skin lesions that are scaly and evolve as polycyclic annular lesions or plaques similar to those of plaque psoriasis.

Ultraviolet Rays - Invisible rays that are part of the energy that comes from the sun and can burn the skin and cause skin cancer.

Whole Food - Food that has been processed or refined as little as possible and is free from additives or other artificial substances.

Connect with the Author

Website: www.shennettesparkes.com
Facebook: Shennette Sparkes
Instagram: _shennettesparkes
Twitter: @coachsheff1908
YouTube: Shennette Sparkes

Made in the USA
Columbia, SC
25 February 2020